Hello Feelings

Written by Poppy O'Neill
Illustrated by Ceej Rowland

Collins

Hello Sadness, it's nice to meet you!
What do you feel like? Can I eat you?

Sometimes sadness feels all misty and foggy,
Like clouds in the sky when it's dark and soggy.

Why do we have to feel sad? Why must that be?
It could be your body saying, "Please hug me!"

Sadness feels hard, it's okay to let it show.
And when it is ready, your sadness will go.

Hello Anger, did we forget you?
Something has happened to upset you!

Anger can be like a volcano, bubbling hot,
Anger can make you do things you wish you
had not.

Everybody gets angry, and sometimes shouts.
Anger feels better with a big breath in, then out.

Anger is quieter now, and ready to say,
"I'd best be off now. See you another day."

Hello Fear, what is that on your shoulder?
Your fears are as heavy as a boulder!

Fear turns you to jelly from head to toe.
Fear makes your pulse race quickly: go, go, go!

Fear is normal, but it's tricky.
Tell your fears, and feel less icky.

Fear is little now, it's going to disappear.
Give it a wave, and say, "See you later, Fear!"

Hello Joy, you're feeling so glad to be alive!
You're like a funny unicorn ready to jive.

Joy feels bouncy, fizzy and fun.
Joy makes you giggle, wiggle and run!

You can spread happy feelings with everyone you meet,
Just smile a big smile when you see them on the street.

Joy is getting tired, it's time to feel something new.
See you another day, Joy. Have fun! Toodle-oo!

Feelings visit for a while, and then drift away.

They float along just like clouds on a windy day.

Feelings don't need to be kept under cover.
We all feel: children, grown-ups, sisters and brothers.

Be kind to all your feelings, let them show.
Cry, speak, wiggle, they're here to help you grow.

When they're ready, feelings will go.
Along will come another, to say hello.

Spotting feelings

Anger

beating quickly

face: red, frowning
body: tense, hot
thinking: it's not fair!

Joy

lots of energy

face: smiling, shiny
body: relaxed, happy
thinking: I am lucky

25

Sadness

tired and sluggish

face: drooping, dull
body: heavy, slow
thinking: everything is terrible and pointless

Fear

on high alert

face: rigid, tense
body: shaky, trembling
thinking: I am not safe

Belly breaths

Deep breaths help your body to relax when you are feeling big feelings.

Place one hand on your belly and take a deep breath in.

Try to push your hand out as your belly gets bigger.

Now let your breath out slowly all the way. Doing this three times can help you focus and begin to cope better with what you are feeling.

Hello feelings

🐾 Review: After reading 🐾

Use your assessment from hearing the children read to choose any GPCs, words or tricky words that need additional practice.

Read 1: Decoding

- Focus the children on words with "y" endings. Ask them to read the following. Ask: Which of these end in an /igh/ or /ee/ sound?
  sky   tricky   fizzy   why   heavy   funny
- Ask the children to take turns to read a verse of the poem. Say: Can you blend in your head when you read the words?

Read 2: Prosody

- Ask the children to look at the punctuation on pages 14 and 15 before taking turns to read a verse aloud.
- Discuss whether they spotted:
  - o the commas: Did you pause?
  - o the exclamation marks: What feeling did you put into these lines?
  - o the apostrophe: Did you remember to read **you're** as one word?
- Bonus content: Ask the children to read pages 28 and 29 as if they are presenting a television programme. Remind them to use emphasis to make the sense clear.

Read 3: Comprehension

- Talk about times when the children have felt sad or angry. What words would they choose to describe the feeling?
- Ask the children what they think is the main message about feelings. Discuss the title and if necessary, revisit pages 20 and 21, and discuss the first line of each page.
- Turn to pages 2 and 3, and focus on the word **like**. Ask the children to reread the text before suggesting a phrase with a similar meaning.
  (e.g. *similar to, the same as*) Talk about how comparisons are often used in poems to describe things.
- Use pages 30 and 31 to encourage the children to identify the feelings and explain the key features of each. Ask:
  - o Which picture shows Anger? Why is it shown as a volcano?
    (e.g. *it makes you feel **bubbling hot***) What can it make us do?
    (e.g. *things you don't want to do, and shout*)
  - o Which picture shows sadness? What does your body need when you're sad? (*a hug*)
  - o What do all these feelings have in common? (e.g. *they drift away*)
- Bonus content: Ask the children to read pages 24 and 25. Challenge them to think of a sentence comparing the feelings. (e.g. *Anger gives you a red, frowning face but Joy makes you smile.*)